# A Mom's Battle Cry To Overcome Fear

Laura J. Marshall

Copyright © 2013 Laura J. Marshall

All rights reserved.

"Scripture taken from the New King James Version®. Copyright © 1982 by Thomas Nelson, Inc. Used by permission. All rights reserved."

THE HOLY BIBLE, NEW INTERNATIONAL VERSION®, NIV® Copyright © 1973, 1978, 1984, 2011 by Biblica, Inc.™ Used by permission. All rights reserved worldwide.

ISBN-13: 978-1482568011
ISBN-10: 1482568012

To Sylvia
Love & Blessings,
Laura Marshall

LAURA J. MARSHALL

## DEDICATION

Dedicated to my friends, who have lifted us in prayer throughout the years and many times, stormed the gates of heaven on behalf of myself and my family.

## ACKNOWLEDGMENTS

With special thanks to Becks Porter for her amazing prayers at the end of each chapter in this book.

With a grateful heart and thanksgiving for my friend, confidant, and editor, Christine Meier Glanzmann for all of her hard work and dedication in working with me on this series.

LAURA J. MARSHALL

## CONTENTS

1 Introduction

2 Day One ~ The Wind

3 Day Two ~ The Clamor of Angels

4 Day Three ~ Sheep Tipping

5 Day Four ~ Satan's Sifting

6 Day Five ~ Take Up Your Weapons

7 Day Six ~ Penny For Your Thoughts

8 Day Seven ~ Chasing Sunbeams

9 In The End

LAURA J. MARSHALL

# INTRODUCTION

When God first brought this book to mind as I wrote the chapter "The Sword" in *A Mom's Battle Cry for Rest*, I resisted the thought. Later, as again it was brought before me, I cried out in my head, "I can't!" That's when I knew. Somewhere deep down, fear still had me in its grip. Though it wasn't somewhere I lived, a part of me was still enslaved.

Several nights later I had dreams of running through a large home, locking the many windows and doors. They didn't seem secure enough or strong enough to keep whatever it was I was afraid of out. It was there. It lurked and watched me. I could see one door was still open, yet it was unreachable. The dogs outside in the yard barked and pawed the ground. They felt the watching, too. Did they sense my fear? I cried deep inside, "I don't want to live there again."

But here I am again. I take this journey with you. Not from the same depths as before, but I climb again and make the ascent.

This is A Mom's Battle Cry to Overcome Fear.

LAURA J. MARSHALL

## DAY ONE ~ THE WIND

I made my way across the lawn to take the neighbor's dog out and feed her lunch. I hadn't really thought about this walk consciously. I take it every weekday, about twice a day. Something heavy hung over me today, though.

I got the dog out of her crate and unlocked the back door. The wind blew and caught the grill cover, thrusting it out and in front of my legs. My heart leapt into my throat; I was scared. Scared to death….of the wind. The movement had caused terror to seize my heart. Had the grill been there before? Something I hadn't given a thought to for days on end loomed large and frightening.

I could have laughed at my ridiculousness had I not wanted to cry at the fear. It was back. What was devastating to me was that it wasn't just something I could gaze at from afar, but it gripped my heart unexpectedly and frightened me to the core. It took me back to the seat of my fears…as a girl, as a woman; so separate, yet connected, and crying out from the corners of my memories….valid and tangible.

And so, I revisit you, Fear. In places in the past and places in the present. I'm there again to take the journey back; back to freedom. This time I know there *is* freedom. I know there *is* hope. I've lived free for a long time now. I've walked empty dark parking lots at 10:30 at night to go to the night shift at a local hospital, fearless.

As I write, God reminds me of the echoes of my earliest fears. As a girl, younger than 5-years-old, I was awoken by a strange man in my room. He had my sister who was two years older, and with little explanation, we were led past my mother's bedroom door to his waiting car. My sister and I sat in the front seat together. It was the middle of the night. I remember feeling cold and seeing lots of cars speeding past us in the darkness. I wanted to yell for help. I don't know if I cried as we drove. I feel we were stoic, my sister and I. I remember a deep abiding fear. Something bad could happen, but it was unnamable in my child's heart. I wanted my mother. Miraculously, in what seems like minutes now on reflection, we were whisked into a hospital and to her side. She had had an allergic reaction to an antibiotic and a neighbor's relative had taken us to the hospital. Had he told us that? Did I just not hear? No matter. Fear had entered my life. It loosely gripped me as I grew.

Fast forward to adulthood, married with children, just two at the time. My oldest son had been sick all day. It was a warm, rainy summer day. There was only one window in our small rental home that was open, the window behind my son's head on the couch.

Throughout the afternoon, a voice kept urging me, "Close the window." I silently and continually cast it off, ignoring it. The voice became more insistent, a little louder, almost like a thought that wasn't mine. Finally, I stopped what I was doing, straightened up and out loud, said just as forcefully, "It is raining. There is only one window open in the house and I am not closing it." The voice stopped.

Satisfied, I continued on with my day. Little did I know the enemy's plans that I would have to fight against that night; the battle God had tried to protect me from. For He Himself has said, "I will never leave you nor forsake you." So we may boldly say, "The Lord is my helper, I will not fear; what can man do to me?"

I put the kids to bed at 7:30, settling myself on the couch to watch some television with a silent prayer for a restful night's sleep for my sons. The doors were locked, and the house cleaned up. As the night wore on, I became restless. I called my husband at work. After saying our goodnights, I started for the bathroom to take a tub. For some reason this night, "something" told me to forego this ritual and read my Bible before going to sleep.

At 10:45, I awoke to a noise. I walked out of my bedroom, glancing into our children's room. All was quiet. As I peered into the living room lit partly by the hallway light hanging overhead, I could make out the back of a man leaning the screen from the open window against the wall. My mind couldn't take in what I was seeing as he turned and faced me. Time seemed to stand still. I said, "What are you doing in my house?" Casually, he walked towards me. Thoughts that something had happened to my husband at work crossed my mind.

The last two feet, he flew at me, grabbing me roughly. I started screaming for help and struggling as he flipped off the light switch and dragged me into the living room. I could hear my children yelling for me. He put his hand over my nose and mouth. I was blacking out. I desperately tried to bite him as I was pushed to the floor. I prayed in my head over and over, "Help me, God!" That still small voice again, "Be Still." I went limp and he pulled his hand off my face.

Gulping in deep breaths of air, I yelled to my children, "Stay in your beds and go to sleep." Silence. The man looked at me saying, "That was smart."

I prayed aloud, pleading prayers to my Father in heaven; only one or two words, four strung together…a continuous prayer up to heaven. In my fear, I cried out to God.

When I think back, I remember those prayers….and my faith. Even unto death, I remember my faith in God to rescue me. I think of my God and His presence and care during that time. Care in the midst of death. I am not a prisoner to the memory, but I can bring myself to the door of fear, open it, enter, and lock myself back in. I'm here to tell you, there is a way to let yourself out of living in the Prison of Fear. If I can do it, you can do it.

There's nothing extraordinary about me. I just have an extraordinary God.

Have you read the story of David and Goliath in 1 Samuel 17? The boy who tended the sheep came into the camp of King Saul to give food to his brothers and the captains of Saul's army. David arrives to find the men afraid of the large Philistine, Goliath. In verse 26, David speaks after hearing about Goliath, "For who is this uncircumcised Philistine that he should defy the armies of the living God?"

David's words were reported to King Saul who then sent for David. In verses 32 through 34, David tells King Saul that he will go fight the Philistine. King Saul tells David he will be unable to fight, since he is just a youth and Goliath a man of war from his youth. David proceeds to tell King Saul how he has rescued lambs from both a bear and a lion.

Verse 37: Moreover David said, "The Lord, who delivered me from the paw of the lion and the paw of the bear, He will deliver me from the hand of this Philistine."

After unsuccessfully trying to don the King's armor, David faces Goliath with the weapons he is familiar with: A sling and five smooth stones....and his faith in God.

Upon facing Goliath, David says in verses 45 through 46, "You come to me with a sword, with a spear, and with a javelin. But I come to you in the name of the

Lord of hosts, the God of the armies of Israel, whom you have defied. This day, The Lord will deliver you into my hand."

Continuing in verse 47, "Then this assembly shall know that the Lord does not save with sword and spear, for the battle is the Lord's and He will give you into our hands."

David takes a stone and slings it. It strikes and sinks into Goliath's forehead and he falls on his face to the earth.

David had faith in God to triumph. David remembered how God was with him at other times in his life and saved him. He trusted in God's continual care. David had faith. God is on your side. We don't need any special weapons. He's already equipped us.

Psalm 91:1-5 reads:

Whoever dwells in the shelter of the Most High
will rest in the shadow of the Almighty.
I will say of the Lord, "He is my refuge and my fortress,
my God, in whom I trust."

Surely he will save you
from the fowler's snare
and from the deadly pestilence.
    He will cover you with his feathers,
and under his wings you will find refuge;
*His faithfulness* will be your shield and rampart.

You will not fear the terror of night, nor the arrow that flies by day.

The scripture above talks of *God's faithfulness*. God is faithful to watch over us. If we, being human, have even a seed of faith in which Jesus spoke in Matthew 17, then we could move a mountain. I can't imagine the *faithfulness of God*. It is too immense a thought for me. I can fathom, though, how in my scattered Mom brain, I can forget to pray over something or someone that's important to me…like my children on a moment-by-moment basis to be safe at school. However, I trust in *God's faithfulness* that when I forget, He doesn't.

"*His faithfulness will be your shield and rampart.*" Rampart is a defensive or protective barrier. He is our shield, our wall of protection. He is faithful to watch over *us*. Whether you *feel* worthy or not of His care, you have it.

When the man who was in my home was leaving, he stood over me and then slowly walked to the front door. He unlocked it and looked back, "Don't call the police or tell anyone. If you do, I'll come back and hurt you and your kids."

He left and I lay there for a moment. My mind was numb. I ran to the door a minute later and shut and locked it, doing the same with the window. I peeked into my children's room to find them sleeping soundly and grabbed the phone, making my way into the bathroom. I took a robe from behind the door and flipped the light on, looking into the mirror.

That night who I was changed forever. What the enemy had meant for evil, in that moment, would be turned around...slowly. I couldn't let someone else suffer as I had due to not speaking up. I had to trust that God would protect us, no matter what I had just gone through. I dialed 911.

God is faithful.

The Wind:

Fear

Faith

The Faithfulness of God

~

Father, as I take this journey to uncover the root of my fears, remind me that I have my faith in You and not in myself. Help me to remember that in You, I am more than a conqueror! That in You, I am restored! And that Your faithfulness to deliver me is a promise I can and will stand on! In Jesus' Name I pray, Amen.

Fear Fighter:

"Then I said to you, 'Do not be terrified, or afraid of them. The Lord your God, who goes before you, He will fight for you, according to all He did for you in Egypt before your eyes, and in the wilderness where you saw how the Lord your God carried you, as a man carries his son, in all the way that you went until you came to this place.'"
Deuteronomy 1:29

LAURA J. MARSHALL

## DAY TWO ~ THE CLAMOR OF ANGELS

Do you believe in angels? I never really gave it much thought and on a daily basis, I really don't, but angels are among us. Good and bad.

After being released from the hospital that night, I lay in the guest room bed at my mother's home. My husband lay next to me. My children were picked up by my brother-in-law while I was at the hospital and were asleep at my sister's house. It was loud, so loud I couldn't sleep. I peeked over my husband's shoulder and wondered why he didn't hear the clamor. I couldn't tell where it was coming from. I sat up slightly in bed and looked across the room. It was as if God opened up my eyes, for there before me was a fierce battle between two warring groups of angels.....not far from the end of my bed!

Hebrews 1:13-14, But to which of the angels has He ever said: "Sit at My right hand, till I make Your enemies Your footstool?" Are they not all ministering spirits sent forth to minister for those who will inherit salvation?

Psalm 91:9-13 reads:

Because you have made the Lord, who is my refuge,
Even the Most High, your dwelling place,
No evil shall befall you,
Nor shall any plague come near your dwelling;
For He shall give *His angels charge over you,*
*To keep you in all your ways.*
In their hands they shall bear you up,
Lest you dash your foot against a stone.
You shall tread upon the lion and the cobra,
The young lion and the serpent you shall trample underfoot.

I don't want to get caught up in *looking for angels*. It's not biblical and it's a distraction. However, God has given the angels tasks and the Bible says one of those is to minister to us. We can have confidence in God to care for us *and* give His angels charge over us, to keep us in all our ways...in the spiritual and in the natural.

2 Kings 6:15-17 reads:

When the servant of the man of God got up and went out early the next morning, an army with horses and chariots had surrounded the city. "Oh no, my lord! What shall we do?" the servant asked.

"Don't be afraid," the prophet answered. "Those who are with us are more than those who are with them."

And Elisha prayed, "Open his eyes, Lord, so that he may see." Then the Lord opened the servant's eyes, and he looked and saw the hills full of horses and chariots of fire all around Elisha.

We never lived in that house again, and stayed with my mother for several months until we purchased a home. I had problems for weeks after my altercation with what is called "posttraumatic stress disorder." I would startle and *fear* would clutch my heart at loud noises. While driving, no matter how much I tried to prepare myself, I would jump when a stoplight changed suddenly from red to green. I knew the light was going to change, and yet, I couldn't prepare enough; my heart would leap into my chest. Fear was *inside* me.

2 Timothy 1:7 reads, For God has not given us a spirit of fear, but of power and of love and of a sound mind.

*The spirit of fearfulness does not come from God.*

At that time, it wasn't often I left the *place of fear*. I lived there. I went to counseling at a local nonprofit organization which dealt with assault survivors. It was there I first heard that I was a survivor and not a victim. It would take several months before I moved from one state and into the other. I was still a victim, looking over my shoulder, purposely staying home at night and during the day. Not long afterwards, I found a Christian counselor and my husband and I both went for a time.

In the days immediately after that night, I went to the police station and worked with a sketch artist. My husband and I also got fingerprinted so that they could rule out our prints as those not on the window screen. I spent several days going through books of suspects and even went along on a stakeout at a local grocery store to look at one suspect in particular with police.

Yes, I was fearful during the process of healing. I was scared to move forward, yet scared to stay where I was. My body, the very cells themselves, felt like they clung to the anguish and fear, whether I wanted them to or not. I get breathless when I go there, even now.

*Fear keeps us focused on ourselves.*

I didn't ask this man to come into my life in this fierce and terrifying way. So what did I do with the fear…..the memories? How did the keys to the door out of that place of fear suddenly appear?

Let's read about Stephen.

Acts 7:54-59 reads:

When the members of the Sanhedrin heard this, they were furious and gnashed their teeth at him. But Stephen, full of the Holy Spirit, looked up to heaven and saw the glory of God, and Jesus standing at the right hand of God. "Look," he said, "I see heaven open and the Son of Man standing at the right hand of God."

At this they covered their ears and, yelling at the top of their voices, they all rushed at him, dragged him out of the city and began to stone him. Meanwhile, the witnesses laid their coats at the feet of a young man named Saul.

While they were stoning him, Stephen prayed, "Lord Jesus, receive my spirit." Then he fell on his knees and cried out, "Lord, do not hold this sin against them." When he had said this, he fell asleep.

*Don't you think that being beaten was terrifying and devastating? What did he do? What did Jesus do in the agony of His suffering?*

Luke 23: 32-34, Two other men, both criminals, were also led out with Jesus to be executed. When they came to the place called the Skull, they crucified him there, along with the criminals—one on his right, the other on his left. Jesus said, "Father, forgive them, for they do not know what they are doing." And they divided up his clothes by casting lots.

*They each prayed for their persecutors. Forgiveness and love prevailed.*

Matthew 6:9-14 reads:

In this manner, therefore, pray:

Our Father in heaven,
Hallowed be Your name.
Your kingdom come.
Your will be done
On earth as it is in heaven.
Give us this day our daily bread.
And forgive us our debts,

As we forgive our debtors.
And do not lead us into temptation,
But deliver us from the evil one.
For Yours is the kingdom and the power and the glory forever. Amen.

"For if you forgive men their trespasses, your heavenly Father will also forgive you. But if you do not forgive men their trespasses, neither will your Father forgive your trespasses.

Along the way, God showed me the remembered prayers of that night and lifted them before me. I was to cling to that symbol…my faith in Him. He also showed me that I was to pray for the man who came into our house. So when fear reared its head, I would pray. Slowly I included this man. Slowly I began to heal.

The Clamor of Angels:

Spiritual forces

Prayer

Forgiveness and Love

Father, I thank You that You have not given me a spirit of fear, but of power, love, and a sound mind! This battle is not against flesh and blood; help me to remember that in the midst of everything. Remind me to pray in those moments. Help me to forgive as You have forgiven. Help me to love as You have loved. Help me to heal, for You are my Healer. In Jesus' Name, I pray, Amen.

Fear Fighter:

This poor man cried out, and the Lord heard him,
And saved him out of all his troubles.
The angel of the Lord encamps all around those who fear Him,
And delivers them.
Psalm 34:6-7

_____
_____
_____
_____
_____
_____
_____
_____
_____
_____
_____
_____
_____
_____
_____
_____
_____
_____
_____
_____
_____
_____
_____
_____
_____

## DAY THREE ~ SHEEP TIPPING

Apparently I didn't do enough to defend myself when the altercation in my home occurred. Was I supposed to run away and leave my children? Over the month immediately following the incident, I actually did have some people question what happened and what I did about it at the time.

This brought back the helplessness I felt and bitterness began to grow; not at people, but at God. *Where were you God? Why does it sound like I fought alone in other people's eyes? I know you were there, weren't you?* I started to question and wonder if I had done enough at the time and if God had.

I became angry and walked away from God for about a year. It wasn't a conscious thing at the time, but the automatic talking and praying to God, I purposely ceased. It was one of the darkest times in my life. I made bad choices. I became depressed and my marriage slowly fell apart. I was dissatisfied with life and angry all the time.

I have found that anger is not far away when fear is in

my life. As I have relived these moments in this book with you, fear has been my companion many days again and anger has come on its heels; anger not only at what happened, but in the here and now. Anger over unreasonable things as fear grasped and clung onto my inward soul. Trust was waning again. It separated me and called me to a place no one could visit, not even God as He gently knocked and beckoned me closer.

It wasn't until towards the end of that year that I realized who I was angry with. Even though He had tried to keep me from it and then got me through the event, I was angry at God for what happened. When the realization hit me, I floundered. *Who was I to be mad at the Living God?*

Fear of God clutched my heart then. It was a well-placed fear. It was a healthy fear.

Psalm 111:10 states: The fear of the Lord is the beginning of wisdom; all who follow his precepts have good understanding. To him belongs eternal praise.

Proverbs 14:26-27 says, Whoever fears the Lord has a secure fortress, and for their children it will be a refuge. The fear of the Lord is a fountain of life, turning a person from the snares of death.

It wasn't many days after that that I cried out to God, literally aloud as I took a tub one night. Crying tears over that fateful night, and all that I had lost since, in the course of my living in a place of fear and anger.

In the Bible, we are described as sheep…the followers of God. I did some research and found that sheep aren't particularly intelligent animals. They also have no sense of direction, so when they wander away from their flock, it's almost impossible for them to find their way back on their own. They are helpless; they have no way of defending themselves.

Luke 15:3-7 reads, Then Jesus told them this parable: "Suppose one of you has a hundred sheep and loses one of them. Doesn't he leave the ninety-nine in the open country and go after the lost sheep until he finds it? And when he finds it, he joyfully puts it on his shoulders and goes home. Then he calls his friends and neighbors together and says, 'Rejoice with me; I have found my lost sheep.' I tell you that in the same way there will be more rejoicing in heaven over one sinner who repents than over ninety-nine righteous persons who do not need to repent.

We are never outside God's grace. Jesus will come after us, putting us gently on his shoulders to carry us home. In the year that I walked away from God, ignoring Him, reminders of Him, and His Word, He pursued me. He never left me. I left Him. I refused to acknowledge Him in my life.

It was like someone had tipped my wooly body over and I couldn't right myself. I was askew. The world looked different. People gathered and pointed at my flailing legs and growing coat of fleece. People. People scared me.

What are your fears? Are they fears of man, the spiritual realm, public places, the death of a loved one? Our fears many times sound foolish to someone else.

In our nursery class at church, I helped the 3- and 4-year-olds make a planter for Easter with live succulents. After church, we had some extra plants and my pastor's wife gave them to me to make a planter with my children at home.

I was excited. The kids and I filled the planter with soil, rocks, the succulent plants, and sticks glued together to make the three crosses of Calvary.

I love and cherish this little planter, but I have anxiety when it comes to house plants. I envy the beautiful plants that people have in their homes; little green treasures with their sprouts reaching towards the sunlight as they line the back of a kitchen sink. I yearn to snip herbs and smell their fragrance as I cook or clean throughout the day. The problem I have is that I tend to kill them and so this fear has taken root.

A foothold.

When I look at the planter sitting cheerfully in the center of my kitchen table, my hands fairly itch to run and get the spray bottle full of water. *Am I watering it too much? Am I not watering it enough?* Fear does grip at me somewhat with this houseplant. I've avoided live plants slowly over the years, as I've learned that once they enter my home, they leave in a trash bag.

*How am I ever going to grow little pots of scented flowers and herbs that cheer up my workspace if they cause me such anxiety?*

A foothold becomes a stronghold. The door has been opened. Even though the "No Solicitors" sign was up and posted for all to see, that thought came and knocked on the door. You opened it and that thought stuck its foot in the door so you couldn't close it while it gave you its sales pitch and invaded your mind. Then it came to stay. It moved in. It became a habit or way of thinking.

When the Israelites sent a party of men to explore the land of Canaan, they returned after 40 days. The men grumbled and gave this account in Numbers 13:

"We went into the land to which you sent us, and it does flow with milk and honey! Here is its fruit. But *the people who live there are powerful, and the cities are fortified and very large.* We even saw descendants of Anak there. The Amalekites live in the Negev; the Hittites, Jebusites and Amorites live in the hill country; and the Canaanites live near the sea and along the Jordan."

*I see fear in the words of the men who explored the land.*

Then Caleb silenced the people before Moses and said, "We should go up and take possession of the land, for we can certainly do it."

*Caleb had confidence in God. Caleb knew God was faithful and bigger than any man or fortified city. God was with them! This was the Promised Land!*

But the men who had gone up with him said, "We can't attack those people; they are stronger than we are." And they spread among the Israelites a bad report about the land they had explored. They said, "The land we explored devours those living in it. All the people we saw there are of great size. We saw the Nephilim there (the descendants of Anak come from the Nephilim). We seemed like grasshoppers in our own eyes, and we looked the same to them."

As a result of not trusting in God, being disobedient and unfaithful (verse 33), only Caleb and Joshua were able to enter the Promised Land…..40 years later.

Don't miss out on your Promised Land! The land God has set aside for you. The land God will conquer for you as you trust in Him. The land that is your inheritance.

What has fear given to you? Or has it just snared, cheated, and robbed you of your promised land? Has it tipped you over and left you flailing?

Take courage! Our God is bigger than the giants of this life. He calms the storms. Have confidence in *who* your God is. Fix your eyes on the Lord.

So He said, "Come." And when Peter had come down out of the boat, he walked on the water to go to Jesus.

But when he saw that the wind was boisterous, he was afraid; and beginning to sink he cried out, saying, "Lord, save me!"

And immediately Jesus stretched out His hand and caught him, and said to him, "O you of little faith, why did you doubt?" And when they got into the boat, the wind ceased. (Matthew 14:29-32)

Sheep Tipping:

Bitterness and Anger

Fear of God

Foothold becomes a Stronghold

The Promised Land

~

Father, I determine to get rid of any and all bitterness and anger in my heart. I don't want it there anymore! I don't want it to have the influence in my life that it has had in the past. Lord, show me where I have allowed the enemy any foothold in my life. Show me where any footholds have become strongholds. Help me to uproot those strongholds! Help me to replace those strongholds with faith and trust in You! In Jesus' Name I pray, Amen

Fear Fighter:

The Lord is my light and my salvation—
   whom shall I fear?
The Lord is the stronghold of my life—
   of whom shall I be afraid?

When the wicked advance against me
   to devour me,
it is my enemies and my foes
   who will stumble and fall.
Though an army besiege me,
   my heart will not fear;
though war break out against me,
   even then I will be confident.
I remain confident of this:
   I will see the goodness of the Lord
   in the land of the living.

Wait for the Lord;
   be strong and take heart
   and wait for the Lord.
Psalm 27:1-3, 14

_____
_____
_____
_____
_____
_____
_____
_____
_____
_____

# DAY FOUR ~ SATAN'S SIFTING

Surely Satan does not speak to God about us in the same way he spoke about Job. Surely not; we are just sheep. Job was a man of great wealth, consequence, and faith.

This is the story as we are told it in Job 1:6-12:

Now there was a day when the sons of God came to present themselves before the Lord, and Satan also came among them. And the Lord said to Satan, "From where do you come?"

So Satan answered the Lord and said, "From going to and fro on the earth, and from walking back and forth on it."

Then the Lord said to Satan, "Have you considered My servant Job, that there is none like him on the earth, a blameless and upright man, one who fears God and shuns evil?"

So Satan answered the Lord and said, "Does Job fear God for nothing? Have You not made a hedge around him, around his household, and around all that he has on every side? You have blessed the work of his hands, and his possessions have increased in the land. But now, stretch out Your hand and touch all that he has, and he will surely curse You to Your face!"

And the Lord said to Satan, "Behold, all that he has is in your power; only do not lay a hand on his person."

So Satan went out from the presence of the Lord.

Most of me wants to be like Job. God pointed him out as an example. He was an upright man. He feared God. He shunned evil. Surely we want to be like Job? Yes? No?

It's who we're being pointed out to that is the fear. It was for me.

*Go away, Satan. Don't consider me. I'm not a threat. Really.*

Has God blessed the work of your hands and given you increase? Has He put a hedge of protection around you and your family? Surely we desire this. We want to duck our heads and avoid confrontation. We want to stay within the hedge and be blessed. We want to live quiet lives without strife or consequence.

Maybe you haven't seen the increase. Have you been hanging on for dear life, sometimes by only one hand that is white and numb from the effort? Some days I feel like this. I struggle. I cling. I run and tuck into the

Father and beg Him for that increase or that protection. Life has tossed me to and fro. There are weeks, months that feel like decades. If you asked me how old I felt, 100 would be too small a number.

Luke 22:31-32 reads, "And the Lord said, "Simon, Simon! Indeed, Satan has asked for you, that he may sift you as wheat. But I have prayed for you, that your faith should not fail; and when you have returned to Me, strengthen your brethren."

What is Satan's goal? What is God's in this?

Satan asks for permission from God because he cannot take you away or cause adversity in your life without God's permission. Satan will ask to sift the Judas', as well as the Peters' and the Jobs'.

Surely God's goal is to shake out the impurities and see if there was really any true faith in us….as He did with Peter and Job. Or perhaps it is for our own growth and maturity or for us to glorify God in our suffering and ultimate restoration? Can there be anything greater in this life than to glorify God?

Strife and consequence can also come as a result of our own choices and not only from Satan's sifting. We can live life sowing to the flesh or sowing to the spirit. For me, unfortunately, many days it's an intermingling of the two. We have free will. Our choices and the choices of those around us ultimately have consequences in both the natural and the spiritual.

Peter writes in 1 Peter 5:6-11:

Humble yourselves, therefore, under God's mighty hand, that he may lift you up in due time. Cast all your anxiety on him because he cares for you.

Be alert and of sober mind. Your enemy the devil prowls around like a roaring lion looking for someone to devour. Resist him, standing firm in the faith, because you know that the family of believers throughout the world is undergoing the same kind of sufferings.

And the God of all grace, who called you to his eternal glory in Christ, after you have suffered a little while, will himself restore you and make you strong, firm and steadfast. To him be the power for ever and ever. Amen.

*The Lord will strengthen us. He will help us to endure, be established, adamant, constant, inflexible, relentless, persevering, resolute, stubborn, sure, true, unflinching, immovable, unwavering, and abiding.*

An abiding faith….

Satan's Sifting:

Satan

God's Purposes

Choices

Father, the enemy may be trying to keep me down, but I am standing firm that You have a plan and a purpose for *me*. Despite the circumstances that, to human eyes, seem hopeless, I am standing on the promise in Your Word that says You will never leave me nor forsake me! Help me to seek Your will in all of my decisions. Help me to not allow fear to be a factor in any decision making. Help me to walk in Your strength and keep my faith and trust in You! In Jesus' Name I pray, Amen.

Fear Fighter:

In all this you greatly rejoice, though now for a little while you may have had to suffer grief in all kinds of trials. These have come so that the proven genuineness of your faith—of greater worth than gold, which perishes even though refined by fire—may result in praise, glory and honor when Jesus Christ is revealed. Though you have not seen him, you love him; and even though you do not see him now, you believe in him and are filled with an inexpressible and glorious joy, for you are receiving the end result of your faith, the salvation of your souls.
1 Peter 1:6-9

_____
_____
_____
_____
_____
_____
_____
_____
_____
_____
_____
_____
_____
_____
_____
_____
_____
_____
_____
_____

## DAY FIVE ~ TAKE UP YOUR WEAPONS

There is a heaviness that hangs over me as I'm visited by spiritual attacks.

Ephesians 6:12 reads, For we do not wrestle against flesh and blood, but against principalities, against powers, against the rulers of the darkness of this age, against spiritual hosts of wickedness in the heavenly places.

Spirits of anger, bitterness, resentment, fear, jealousy, death, lust, greed visit and cling. And so I trudge along, my head down most days. I feel the weight and I wonder why I can't move forward. Strife hangs over the household, peace flees, children fight, and unease prevails. I come up for air. I look around and recognize what is clinging to us. My spiritual eyes have been opened and I lift those eyes up to my Savior.

Continuing in Ephesians 6 to verse 13, Therefore take up the whole armor of God, that you may be able to withstand in the evil day, and having done all, to stand.

I take up my weapons.

Verses 14-20, Stand therefore, having girded your waist with truth, having put on the breastplate of righteousness, and having shod your feet with the preparation of the gospel of peace; above all, taking the shield of faith with which you will be able to quench all the fiery darts of the wicked one. And take the helmet of salvation, and the sword of the Spirit, which is the Word of God; praying always with all prayer and supplication in the Spirit, being watchful to this end with all perseverance and supplication for all the saints.

I pray aloud, rebuking in Jesus' name these spirits. Yes, I have anointed my home with oil, each room and doorway….sometimes a pillow; anything I feel led to anoint, including myself. There are 93 scriptures in the Bible that pertain to anointing oil. Here are a few:

James 5:14, Is anyone among you sick? Let him call for the elders of the church, and let them pray over him, anointing him with oil in the name of the Lord.

Mark 6:13, And they cast out many demons, and anointed with oil many who were sick, and healed them.

Exodus 40:9, And you shall take the anointing oil, and anoint the tabernacle and all that is in it; and you shall hallow it and all its utensils, and it shall be holy.

Matthew 6:17, But you, when you fast, anoint your head and wash your face.

I have had close friends join with me in prayer over

particularly tough things spiritually that no amount of fasting, anointing, or prayers were moving. When they join with me in prayer, the spirit has lifted immediately.

Matthew 18:19-20 reads, Again, truly I tell you that if two of you on earth agree about anything they ask for, it will be done for them by my Father in heaven. For where two or three gather in my name, there am I with them.

Our weapons have substance in the spiritual realm. Throughout scripture we see how prayers, fasting, faith, and the Word of God are our offense and defense.

When David went to fight Goliath, he didn't fit into King Saul's armor. 1 Samuel 17:38-40 reads, Saul said to David, "Go, and the Lord be with you." Then Saul dressed David in his own tunic. He put a coat of armor on him and a bronze helmet on his head. David fastened on his sword over the tunic and tried walking around, because he was not used to them.

"I cannot go in these," he said to Saul, "because I am not used to them." So he took them off. Then he took his staff in his hand, chose five smooth stones from the stream, put them in the pouch of his shepherd's bag and, with his sling in his hand, approached the Philistine.

There is a lesson in this. Wear the armor you're used to as you battle this day. I have friends that are gifted in prayer, strong prayers of war that they speak out in confidence and boldness. I have friends who are quiet, but sing a song of praise or worship that could make you cry and lift a weary countenance. We all have our armor that God has fit to our frames. That's not to say we can't grow into garments as we grow in our faith. Wherever you are NOW, you are equipped to stand firm and fight, whether it is in your prayers and petitions before God, faith, reading the Word, or songs of praise.

In the Old Testament, the Moabites and the Ammonites with some of the Meunites came to wage war against Jehoshaphat. Jehoshaphat prayed at the temple of the Lord in front of the assembly of Judah and Jerusalem. It is a moving prayer, reminding the people and God himself of His mighty hand and how he drove the inhabitants from the land previously for the descendants of Abraham. After his prayer, the Spirit of the Lord came on Jahaziel, son of Zechariah as he stood in the assembly. This is what Jahaziel says in 2 Chronicles 20:15-17, "This is what the Lord says to you: 'Do not be afraid or discouraged because of this vast army. For the battle is not yours, but God's. Tomorrow march down against them. They will be climbing up by the Pass of Ziz, and you will find them at the end of the gorge in the Desert of Jeruel. You will not have to fight this battle. Take up your positions; stand firm and see the deliverance the Lord will give you, Judah and Jerusalem. Do not be afraid; do not be discouraged. Go out to face them tomorrow, and the Lord will be with you.'"

And in verses 21-22, After consulting the people, Jehoshaphat appointed men to sing to the Lord and to praise him for the splendor of his holiness as they went out at the head of the army, saying "Give thanks to the Lord, for his love endures forever."

As they began to *sing and praise*, the Lord set ambushes against the men of Ammon and Moab and Mount Seir who were invading Judah, and they were defeated.

*The power of praise.*

Take Up Your Weapons:

Spiritual Attacks

Anointing with Oil

Weapons

Prayer/Agreement

Praise

Father, remind me that You have given me full armor to put on each day. In the midst of an attack, help me to remember that You have also given me weapons; weapons of anointing oil, fasting, praise, prayer and Your Word. Help me to use those weapons without hindrance. Help me to pull them out the moment I am attacked. Help me to remember that You are my Strength and Shield. I do not need to hide! I can stand firm! In Jesus' Name I pray, Amen.

# A MOM'S BATTLE CRY TO OVERCOME FEAR

Fear Fighter:

Praise the Lord, my soul.

I will praise the Lord all my life;
    I will sing praise to my God as long as I live.
Do not put your trust in princes,
    in human beings, who cannot save.
When their spirit departs, they return to the ground;
    on that very day their plans come to nothing.
Blessed are those whose help is the God of Jacob,
    whose hope is in the Lord their God.

He is the Maker of heaven and earth,
    the sea, and everything in them—
    he remains faithful forever.
He upholds the cause of the oppressed
    and gives food to the hungry.
The Lord sets prisoners free,
    the Lord gives sight to the blind,
the Lord lifts up those who are bowed down,
    the Lord loves the righteous.
The Lord watches over the foreigner
    and sustains the fatherless and the widow,
    but he frustrates the ways of the wicked.

The Lord reigns forever,
    your God, O Zion, for all generations.
Psalm 146

_____
_____
_____
_____

## DAY SIX ~ PENNY FOR YOUR THOUGHTS

During my time of therapy, I was taught a technique to stop a fearful thought midway. I learned to yell, "Stop" in my head. At first, the therapist had me yell it out in her office. I wasn't very good at it, being somewhat shy, but the seed was planted. I practiced in my car alone. I would scream, "Stop!" at the top of my lungs. I tried it when a frightening thought assailed me. I was stopping the thought midway. It was working. I could stop these thoughts when I realized which way they were veering. Having practiced in the car, I could bring forth that memory, that recalled loud yell, and think, "Stop!" *in my head* when I was home with my children or out in public.

Romans 12:1-2 reads, I beseech you therefore, brethren, by the mercies of God, that you present your bodies a living sacrifice, holy, acceptable to God, which is your reasonable service. 2 And do not be conformed to this world, but *be transformed by the renewing of your mind*, that you may prove what is that good and acceptable and perfect will of God.

If a thought lingered or continually assailed me, I would envision myself picking it up and casting it towards the feet of Jesus. Each thought as it came, yelling, "Stop!" in my head and casting it up in prayer.

*Here, please take this, Lord.*

If each thought of fear, anxiety, or worry were a penny, how much would they be worth?

*Too many cares. Too much fear.*

Along the way, I incorporated a saying into my battle plan, which was, "Do not give it a thought".

2 Corinthians 10:3-6 says, For though we walk in the flesh, we do not war according to the flesh. For the weapons of our warfare are not carnal but mighty in God for pulling down strongholds, *casting down arguments* and every high thing that exalts itself against the knowledge of God, *bringing every thought into captivity to the obedience of Christ.*

Take every thought captive to obey Christ. Bring all of your fears and thoughts that are not of God to the feet of Jesus; cast them down. In the fight and flight moments, the body's chemical reaction may take over. Pray. Ask for help and wisdom. He will be there, unto death.

The other day, I was driving the car and I heard a very loud buzzing in the back seat. Over the past year, I have had two experiences where large bees have flown into the car. Those memories assailed me as I drove. I was so distracted and worried over the sound that I swerved into the oncoming lane. I righted the car, looking for somewhere to pull over. Houses lined the narrow street with nowhere to pull off. I heard the buzz again, closer to the back of my head now. I was so scared that I took my eyes off the road and looked back, again swerving into the other lane. (I was so grateful that during both of these times that no cars were coming the other way.)

Reason returned. I remembered my lessons, what we've been talking about in this book: Taking my thoughts back, giving my anxieties and fears to Jesus and leaving them there. I prayed. It calmed my nerves. I drove straight. I didn't look back. The buzzing ceased. I didn't give it another thought. I got to the grocery store, completely forgetting to look around in the car for the source of my fears. Here it is two days later, and I realize I never gave it a care or worry again. Jesus took it, that drive into oncoming traffic body reaction and mind-numbing fear, and worked it out.

I worry and fear over late buses or when my children run outside without me as I finish the dishes. *Make me wise, Father. Make me aware of danger, but not to fear for I trust in your constant continual care over my children and our lives.*

In the free dictionary online, *danger* is defined as the state of being vulnerable to injury, loss, or evil; risk. A person or thing that may cause injury, pain, etc. I found it interesting that the word danger was derived from the

Latin form of dominium/dominus which means sovereignty, lord, and master.

Let us not let danger be the master of our lives. There will always *be* danger. However, it does not have to rule or have dominion over us.

In the little worries of life, in our todays and tomorrows (the beginning footholds), seek God. Trust God. I have security. No matter what happens, He is with me. He is with us. He stands guard and sends His angels forth. He is my hedge of protection and strong tower where I run.

DO NOT GIVE IT A THOUGHT. Examine it. Recognize it. Pray for discernment. Do not think on it for one minute if it stems from fear. Give it to the Lord to carry.

And so I breathe…and pray. I surrender anxious thoughts. I make wise choices and decisions.

Isaiah 26:3 says, You will keep him in perfect peace, Whose mind is stayed on You.

Listen to the voice of the Holy Spirit. The seemingly innocuous whispers of "tie your shoe," "lock your car door," or even…"close the window."

How do we differentiate between the voice of the Holy Spirit versus the voice of a different spirit? The fruits of the Holy Spirit are love, peace, faithfulness, joy, goodness, gentleness, patience, kindness, and self-control.

Test the spirits. Do they reflect what the Word says about the spirit of God? Is there fear, bullying, anger, an urgency to the spirit?

1 Corinthians 13:4-8 says, Love is patient, love is kind. It does not envy, it does not boast, it is not proud. It does not dishonor others, it is not self-seeking, it is not easily angered, it keeps no record of wrongs. Love does not delight in evil but rejoices with the truth. It always protects, always trusts, always hopes, always perseveres. Love never fails.

1 John 4:13-16 reads, God is love. Whoever lives in love lives in God, and God in them. This is how love is made complete among us so that we will have confidence on the day of judgment: In this world we are like Jesus. There is no fear in love. But perfect love drives out fear, because fear has to do with punishment. The one who fears is not made perfect in love.

Penny for Your Thoughts:

Stop!

Casting our Fears/Worry/Anxiety up to the feet of Jesus

Our Thoughts

The Spirit of God

Father, when I am bombarded with thoughts that bring me down and try to drag me back to places I don't want to be, give me the strength to yell, "STOP!" Help me to remember that I don't have to entertain them. Remind me to cast ALL of my fears and worries at Your feet. Remind me to not just take every thought captive, but to replace those thoughts with ones that are true, right, lovely, and of good report. Instead, bring about the promises You have spoken to me through Your Word. May the words of my mouth and the meditations of my heart be acceptable unto You, dear Lord!! In Jesus' Name I pray, Amen.

Fear Fighter:

Consequently, you are no longer foreigners and strangers, but fellow citizens with God's people and also members of his household, built on the foundation of the apostles and prophets, with Christ Jesus himself as the chief cornerstone. In him the whole building is joined together and rises to become a holy temple in the Lord. And in him you too are being built together to become a dwelling in which God lives by his Spirit. Ephesians 2:19-22

## DAY SEVEN ~ CHASING SUNBEAMS

God has given us boundaries in this life. That's what the 10 Commandments were all about. As parents, we set boundaries for our children. "Stay in the yard." "Don't run into the street to chase the ball!" "Don't talk to strangers."

I am sure I have instilled my fair share of fear into my own children over the years, as I've struggled to find my way out of the life-taking, grasping, coiled fears that had taken over the moments and days of my life. Even in recent years, worry has been my companion and caution my melody.

As I was reading the bible recently, a piece of scripture bounced from the page and clung to me to carry and consider. Zephaniah 3:13 says, "And no one shall make them afraid." This speaks of a time when the Lord gathers the nations to the assembly of kingdoms, a time in the future.

There are things here that will *make us afraid*.

We are on earth. It is far from perfect. Far from

heaven. If you're a Christian, it is far from home. Philippians 3:20 reads, For our citizenship is in heaven, from which we also eagerly wait for the Savior, the Lord Jesus Christ.

When I hear a noise at night and fear causes the very blood in my veins to jump, I pray for wisdom and not fear to rule. Fear causes loss. I don't want such loss in my children's lives. I want to instill wisdom into the: A healthy respect for guns; wisdom to stay close in a large city or at a rest stop as we travel on vacation.

*Is there such a thing as a healthy fear?*

Other than fear of God, there is no healthy fear.

*What about anxiety and worry?*

Let's look at Peter, who walked on the water in Matthew 14:29-31.

So He said, "Come." And when Peter had come down out of the boat, he walked on the water to go to Jesus. But when he saw that the wind was boisterous, he was afraid; and beginning to sink he cried out, saying, "Lord, save me!"

And immediately Jesus stretched out His hand and caught him, and said to him, "O you of little faith, why did you doubt?" And when they got into the boat, the wind ceased.

When Peter became afraid, he began to sink. He was

anxious and worried. What did he do? He called out to Jesus. If we lose our focus, we can cry out to God and He will catch us and restore us.

Proverbs 25:28, Whoever has no rule over his own spirit is like a city broken down, without walls.

*We must take rule over our own spirit and flesh.....our weaknesses and our natural tendency to sin.*

Ephesians 2:1-3 reads, And you He made alive, who were dead in trespasses and sins, in which you once walked according to the course of this world, according to the prince of the power of the air, the spirit who now works in the sons of disobedience, among whom also we all once conducted ourselves in the lusts of our flesh, fulfilling the desires of the flesh and of the mind, and were by nature children of wrath, just as the others.

Prepare for the tests, because there will be many. Stay connected to Jesus. In John 15, Jesus refers to Himself as the vine and us as the branches, saying apart from Him we can do nothing. It also says if we abide with Christ, He will abide with us. Having a relationship with Jesus is more important than what we do or don't do.

God will use us in the shadowy places, wherever He has placed us or where we find ourselves.

In Matthew 16:18, Jesus says to Peter, "I will build My church, and the gates of Hades shall not prevail against it."

*Don't let worry or anxiety have dominion over your life.*

Rainbows appear *after* the rain. A baby is born only *through* pain and suffering. Grapes must be *crushed* to make wine. Diamonds are *formed* under extreme pressure. Life isn't wrapped neatly in pretty colorful paper and dressed in shiny bows. What do we miss if we're always chasing sunbeams?

*Be willing to trust God and face something bigger than yourself, despite the fear that lingers.*

Psalm 23:4-5 reads,

Yea, though I walk through the valley of the shadow of death,
I will fear no evil;
For You are with me;
Your rod and Your staff, they comfort me.

You prepare a table before me in the presence of my enemies;
You anoint my head with oil;
My cup runs over.

Circumstances, danger, fears, worry, anxiety can either overwhelm and paralyze you or spur you forward to *walk through* that valley even in the shadow of death. Be brave.

Fear no evil. God is with you. You will eat and be satisfied, even in the presence of your enemies. Your cup will overflow with God's blessings.

Exodus 14:10-22:

And when Pharaoh drew near, the children of Israel lifted their eyes, and behold, the Egyptians marched after them. So they were very afraid, and the children of Israel cried out to the Lord. Then they said to Moses, "Because there were no graves in Egypt, have you taken us away to die in the wilderness? Why have you so dealt with us, to bring us up out of Egypt? Is this not the word that we told you in Egypt, saying, 'Let us alone that we may serve the Egyptians'? For it would have been better for us to serve the Egyptians than that we should die in the wilderness."

*We must get to a point in our walk where we love the Lord more than our own lives.*

And Moses said to the people, "Do not be afraid. Stand still, and see the salvation of the Lord, which He will accomplish for you today. For the Egyptians whom you see today, you shall see again no more forever. The Lord will fight for you, and you shall hold your peace."

*Be still. Steadfast. God will fight the battle for you.*

And the Lord said to Moses, "Why do you cry to Me? Tell the children of Israel to go forward. But lift up your rod, and stretch out your hand over the sea and divide it. And the children of Israel shall go on dry ground through the midst of the sea. And I indeed will harden the hearts of the Egyptians, and they shall follow them. So I will gain honor over Pharaoh and over all his army, his chariots, and his horsemen. Then the Egyptians shall know that I am the Lord, when I have gained honor for Myself over Pharaoh, his chariots, and his horsemen."

*Move forward. Walk through the midst of the sea.*

And the Angel of God, who went before the camp of Israel, moved and went behind them; and the pillar of cloud went from before them and stood behind them. So it came between the camp of the Egyptians and the camp of Israel. Thus, it was a cloud and darkness to the one, and it gave light by night to the other, so that the one did not come near the other all that night.

*The Lord's protection.*

Then Moses stretched out his hand over the sea; and the Lord caused the sea to go back by a strong east wind all that night, and made the sea into dry land, and the waters were divided. So the children of Israel went into the midst of the sea on the dry ground, and the waters were a wall to them on their right hand and on their left.

*Believe and trust God. Your Red Sea moment will come.*

David faced the giant.

Daniel faced the lions.

Shadrach, Meshach, and Abednego faced the fire.

Abraham faced the loss of his son.

Face *your* fears.

2 Corinthians 4:16-18 reads, Therefore we do not lose heart. Even though our outward man is perishing, yet the inward man is being renewed day by day. For our light affliction, which is but for a moment, is working for us a far more exceeding and eternal weight of glory, while we do not look at the things which are seen, but at the things which are not seen. For the things which are seen are temporary, but the things which are not seen are eternal.

Chasing Sunbeams:

Boundaries

Healthy Fear of God

Rule Over Your Flesh

Be Brave

Walk Through

Face Your Fears

Father, thank You for the boundaries You have given me. Help me to remember that You have not given me those boundaries so that I *will* be afraid of things, but so that I don't *have* to be afraid….and that even though the world can be a scary place, I have nothing to fear! My circumstances may seem like crashing waves all around me, but You are there with me in the midst! As long as I keep my eyes on You I cannot sink. Lord, give me the strength to not give in to my flesh, but to make the choices that would help me to grow closer to You. In Jesus' Name I pray, Amen.

# A MOM'S BATTLE CRY TO OVERCOME FEAR

Fear Fighter:

When hard pressed, I cried to the Lord;
   he brought me into a spacious place.
The Lord is with me; I will not be afraid.
   What can mere mortals do to me?
The Lord is with me; he is my helper.
   I look in triumph on my enemies.

It is better to take refuge in the Lord
   than to trust in humans.
It is better to take refuge in the Lord
   than to trust in princes.
All the nations surrounded me,
   but in the name of the Lord I cut them down.
They surrounded me on every side,
   but in the name of the Lord I cut them down.
They swarmed around me like bees,
   but they were consumed as quickly as burning thorns;
   in the name of the Lord I cut them down.
I was pushed back and about to fall,
   but the Lord helped me.
The Lord is my strength and my defense;
   he has become my salvation.
Psalm 118:5-14

_____
_____
_____
_____
_____
_____
_____

## IN THE END

Many years later and several states away, we received a phone call from the same police officer that assisted us throughout the investigation. She had personally traveled to arrest the man who committed the crime. Her words were reassuring, "He admitted it."

How did they find him all that time later?

I was to learn that my case and one other were two of the first cases in that state to lead to a conviction of a crime through DNA.

That little voice in the hospital that night, quietly in my head saying, "Have the doctor swab there."

I was frightened, fairly numb as they administered the assault kit. Yet, I listened and obeyed. Speaking up when I wanted to hide.

The weighty significance of such a small request.

The case went before a judge. There was no trial by jury due to his plea. A cold sweat seized me as the man was led into court; my hands became slick. I struggled. I spoke. Up to 20 years was the sentence.

I was handed a letter he wrote before we left the courthouse. I read it once. He didn't accept full responsibility, placing the blame on alcohol. My prayers over the intervening years felt fruitless in that moment. Having prayed for his salvation, but seeing no repentance.

Yet, God has reminded me. Like the clinging of a favorite perfume, holding up the prayers of that night. In the dark and cloying evil that permeated my living room, God was there. He didn't leave me. His angels were about my children. His care was palpable. It even gave the perpetrator pause. I saw it in his eyes.

The fear of God. The fear of *My* God.

That is the healthy fear. I will stand on His word and within His shadow of loving care.

I trusted God not to forget me. Not for me, but for *who He is* and all that He has promised.

Like I said, "There's nothing extraordinary about me. I just have an extraordinary God."

Hebrews 12:1-3 Therefore we also, since we are surrounded by so great a cloud of witnesses, let us lay aside every weight, and the sin which so easily ensnares us, and let us run with endurance the race that is set before us, looking unto Jesus, the author and finisher of our faith, who for the joy that was set before Him endured the cross, despising the shame, and has sat down at the right hand of the throne of God. For consider Him who endured such hostility from sinners against Himself, lest you become weary and discouraged in your souls.

~

Father, thank You for always being there with me, even in the darkest places and times. Lord, thank You that You are faithful to not only love me where I am, but to care so deeply for me that You don't want me to stay there. As I take these steps towards healing, forgiving and trusting in You, remind me each time of how far I have come from the beginning. Help me to forgive. Help me to stand on Your Word and Your promises to me. Remind me that You have given me the authority and power to stop any thoughts that attack me. Help me to cast ALL of my fears and worries to You. Help me to praise You in the midst. Remind me to put on my full armor and take out my weapons. Lord, I thank You that this battle is not mine. Thank You that You are fighting on my behalf. I am more than a conqueror! Fear has no place in my life! Fear is bound. Peace is loosed. I will stand firm! I will overcome! You are my Strength! You are my Shield! I praise Your Mighty Name! In Jesus' Name I pray, Amen.

Fear Fighter:

Hebrews 12:1-3, Therefore we also, since we are surrounded by so great a cloud of witnesses, let us lay aside every weight, and the sin which so easily ensnares us, and let us run with endurance the race that is set before us, looking unto Jesus, the author and finisher of our faith, who for the joy that was set before Him endured the cross, despising the shame, and has sat down at the right hand of the throne of God. For consider Him who endured such hostility from sinners against Himself, lest you become weary and discouraged in your souls.

# ABOUT THE AUTHOR

Laura J. Marshall lives in Virginia. She writes fiction and nonfiction. You can find out more about Laura and her other books online on her website at www.LauraJMarshall.com. *A Mom's Battle Cry to Love & Be Loved* (excerpt enclosed) and *A Mom's Battle Cry for Health & Beauty* will be releasing in 2013 along with her fiction novella, *Persistent Love*.

LAURA J. MARSHALL

## A Mom's Battle Cry to Love & Be Loved

### Excerpt

### By Laura J. Marshall

1 Corinthians 13:11-13 reads, When I was a child, I spoke as a child, I understood as a child, I thought as a child; but when I became a man, I put away childish things. For now we see in a mirror, dimly, but then face to face. Now I know in part, but then I shall know just as I also am known. And now abide faith, hope, love, these three; but the greatest of these is love.

If the greatest of these is love then I am failing to live as Jesus would have me live. I am failing to love fully. I can feel it. I hold myself back. I am spoken to, but don't answer. I curl in on myself more and more each day…away from my husband, away from myself.

Do you have a pretty little brick house?

The walls are high and thick, covered with beautiful climbing vines. Cool to the touch both inside and out. Even on the hottest of days.

You can see the gardens surrounding the house from quite far away, lush and well cared for. Tulips bloom year-round and the heads of the sunflowers reach high up to the sun. There's an abundance of wildflowers tended by a handsome man. I see him from my window, watering and planting. Carefully trying to find and pull the weeds. Sometimes he even grafts a new flower to brighten my view.

Today, he came to the door to show me some lovely yellow roses. I waved to him from my window....I wish I could have smelled them or let him in but you see there is no handle on the inside.

I look out of different windows every day, some high, some low. Sometimes I stretch and reach to pluck a blossom. On occasion, I can just catch the sound of the nearby brook babbling happily over rocks.

The walls are a cool blue inside. There is a chair next to mine with waiting slippers for your feet and softly muted thick rugs beneath. I would pour us hot tea if you came, to take away the chill.

I do have guests, you know....friends who have found

keys hanging high near the sill on the outside. God has come and stayed a few times. He always leaves the door open. Sunshine pours in. Birds scatter near the doorway, eating crumbs that have fallen from the table. My children live here more times than not. The room is brightly colored as we play or talk.

I am alone a lot looking into the tiny mirrors that cover the walls.....reflecting, reflecting always distorted images. When God visits, He insists on bringing his own mirror. It is beautiful, tall and wide. Its depths of color are unending. I look flawless and perfect. Jesus is always between the mirror and I, visiting too.

So, please come visit my little brick house. Maybe I will let you in or you can come and say hello to the man outside. Tell him I love him and one day we will live in a large house, all of us together. Until that day, he tends and waters and searches. There are days he leaves the garden and I am afraid he won't come back. He is so sad when he sees my friends enter and he cannot.

God has been staying longer and the little mirrors are slowly becoming unglued. One of these days my pretty little brick house will crumble.

This is A Mom's Battle Cry to Love & Be Loved.

LAURA J. MARSHALL

# A MOM'S BATTLE CRY TO OVERCOME FEAR

LAURA J. MARSHALL

# A MOM'S BATTLE CRY TO OVERCOME FEAR

Made in the USA
Charleston, SC
24 April 2013